The
Treasure Trunk

The Treasure Trunk

by Bianca Covelli Stewart
illustrated by Donna Ayers

SIMON & SCHUSTER BOOKS FOR YOUNG READERS

Published by Simon & Schuster

New York · London · Toronto · Sydney · Tokyo · Singapore

E

This book is lovingly dedicated to my family; in particular to my husband, Phil, whose encouragement, patience, and assistance helped to make it a reality.   B.C.S.

Dedicated with love to my family and friends.   D.A.

SIMON & SCHUSTER BOOKS FOR YOUNG READERS
Simon & Schuster Building, Rockefeller Center, 1230 Avenue of the Americas, New York, New York 10020. Text
Copyright © 1991 by Bianca C. Stewart. Illustrations Copyright © 1991 by Donna Ayers. All rights reserved including
the right of reproduction in whole or in part in any form. SIMON & SCHUSTER BOOKS FOR YOUNG READERS is a trademark of
Simon & Schuster Inc. Manufactured in Singapore.
10   9   8   7   6   5   4   3   2   1

Library of Congress Cataloging-in-Publication Data. Stewart, Bianca C. The treasure trunk / by Bianca C. Stewart ;
illustrated by Donna Ayers. Summary: In 1898 in Heightstown, New York, a young woman on the eve of her wedding
reviews the keepsakes of the happy times and holidays spent with her childhood sweetheart. ISBN 0-671-69203-8.
[1. Weddings—Fiction.   2. United States—Social life and customs—19th century—Fiction.]   I. Ayers, Donna, ill.
II. Title. [DNLM: 1. Holidays—Fiction.]   PZ7.S84873Tr   1991   [Fic]—dc20   90-10090

Mr. and Mrs. Benjamin Pendergast
joyfully announce
the marriage of their daughter
Elizabeth Claire
to
Mr. Andrew Winthrop.
The wedding ceremony will be celebrated
on February 14, in the year of our Lord 1898.
The service will take place in
Christ the King Church, Heightstown, New York
at twelve o'clock noon.

A reception will immediately follow
at The Wellington Manor on Willowbrook Lane.

Respondez S'il Vous Plait

Wedding Eve

Andrew and I have known each other nearly all of our lives. I find it difficult to realize that this is the last night that I shall sleep in my parents' home in the bedroom of my childhood. My belongings are packed and ready to be moved into the home I shall share with my old friend, Andrew, who will soon become my husband. As I have sorted through the souvenirs of my girlhood, I have found treasures that link my life with Andrew's through all the years we have grown together. I have put them all into this trunk, a treasure trunk where there is room for all those yet to come.

Easter

The first time Andrew and I saw each other was on Easter Sunday, 1884. His family had just moved into town the week before, and his parents had brought Andrew and his two little sisters to the Easter egg roll on the town commons. The adults and the older children watched as we younger ones played our games and collected the brightly colored eggs in our baskets. The little girls' baskets were trimmed with ribbons to match their dresses. The ribbons on mine were silky, pale yellow. My basket was small, almost too small to hold my eggs and all those Andrew impulsively poured from his basket into mine. Those were his very first gifts to me. I looked into his earnest, generous face and knew immediately that I loved him, that I would always love him. The basket is gone, but the pale yellow ribbon is scarcely faded. I have it still, here in my treasure trunk.

Arbor Day

Andrew entered our school that spring. Since September, we students had been bringing in our pennies with which the headmaster had bought a young tree to be planted on the school grounds on April 22, Arbor Day. As a gesture of welcome and friendship each year, the newest boy in school was chosen to plant the new tree. That year the privilege was Andrew's. The girl who had read the greatest number of books from the school library was selected each year to give the tree its first drink. That year the honor was mine.

Andrew took the young tree into his hands and gently set it into the place prepared for it. Carefully I darkened the earth around its roots with its first drink, which I poured from a small blue and white enamel sprinkling can my mother had bought for the occasion.

The can is chipped at the spout, but I have it still, here in my treasure trunk.

A Picnic

Our parents soon become good friends, too. Our families spent many happy afternoons together sharing picnics along the edge of the lake. Our mothers would bring huge baskets of fried chicken, biscuits, potato salad, homemade pickles and angel food cake. For a dime we could buy a ride in a swan boat and glide merrily on the glass-clear water for an hour.

The first year Andrew was old enough, he joined the boys' bicycle races and won the silver medal for the junior boys. I saw him whisper to his mother, and she smiled and nodded. Shyly, he walked over to me and placed his beautiful prize into my hand. I have it still, here in my treasure trunk.

JULY 4, 1890

SMITHERS TAXES

Independence Day

Independence Day was always a glorious event. The town parade was bright with the red, white and blue uniforms of the band and their shining instruments blazing in the hot July sun. Andrew played the drum and led the marching boys down the center of town. Brave men, like our fathers who were volunteer firemen, rode on the town pumpers.

Their high stepping horses seemed to know how grand they looked with their harnesses decorated for the parade. Speeches from town dignitaries, music, games and picnics filled the afternoon with good cheer. Overhead were wonderful hot air balloons, thirteen of them to represent our first thirteen colonies.

As soon as it grew dark enough, we would abandon our games and settle down on the soft grass to marvel at the fireworks that lit the night sky for miles around.

The year that I was ten, Andrew won the sack race and received a miniature American flag which he gave to me. Its stand is missing, but its colors are as bright as my memories of that day. I have it still, here in my treasure trunk.

At the Beach

For the month of August each year, our families rented houses on the beach along the New Jersey shore. Those glowing, dreamlike days were never long enough. Early each morning, as our mothers sat with their embroidery under a large rose umbrella, we children ran happily along the shore. We built enormous sand castles and dug holes as deep as our arms could reach. Our greatest delight was to splash in and out of the teasing waves. At noon, we would return to our homes to escape the midday sun, eat a cool lunch, and rest for a time. Later in the afternoon we would meet again to walk along the beach and gather the loveliest of the sea shells, rocks and bits of sea glass. Many are the gracefully curved and delicately colored gifts which the sea gave to the land, and which Andrew gave to me. I have some still, here in my treasure trunk.

Apple Picking

It became a tradition for our families to welcome in the autumn season by joining together for an afternoon of apple picking. My father would hire a hay wagon and we would all ride out to the country orchards. While our parents sat at tables drinking freshly made apple cider, we children busied ourselves at the trees. The older boys carried the baskets while we filled them with the smooth, fragrant fruit, still warm from the sun. The youngest children scooped the apples from the lower limbs, but I always tried to reach those nestled high in the tree. It was then that Andrew would come and gently hold down a branch so that I could reach the apple I was determined to pick. By noon the picking was finished and we returned home with our bushels of sweet smelling apples for an afternoon of baking.

All the girls and ladies of our families would spend the rest of the day turning the apples into spicy cakes, creamy puddings and deep-dish pies. Every one had a job to do. The smaller girls would stand on little stools around the butcher-block table so they could stir together the flour and eggs and sugar. The older girls would cut and peel the apples. I was proud and happy the year I was finally counted among those who put all the wonderful smells and tastes into the oven. Andrew's mother always used an old family recipe which she prized and guarded. I knew she really liked me the year she brought me a copy of it. I shall take it with me into my own kitchen. I have it still, here in my treasure trunk.

Halloween

Halloween was a delightful day for the children of our town. At four o'clock in the afternoon, we would gather at the flagpole in the park, then parade to the firehouse which had been transformed into a halloween fairyland. Jack-o-lanterns grinned in the windows, paper bats swung from the rafters, and friendly white-sheeted, ghosts welcomed us inside. There were games like the witches broom dance and apple bobbing. Best of all, there were prizes for the costumes that were the prettiest, the most original, the funniest, and the one that best disguised its wearer. One year, someone arrived in a suit of armor that had been patiently crafted out of fabric and painted silver. Helmet shut tight and without speaking, the knight walked among us, unrecognized, until that warm, steady gaze met mine. I knew immediately that it was Andrew, but I said nothing because I wanted him to win. When he had been awarded his prize, a metal bank shaped like a black cat, he brought it to me and said, smiling, "You knew me all the time. This should be yours." I have it still, here in my treasure trunk.

Thanksgiving

On Thanksgiving Day, our families would gather in Andrew's home. A welcoming fire sang in the fireplace, and the sounds of talk and laughter flowed from the busy kitchen where all the girls congregated to assist Cook with the preparation of the feast. The tantalizing aromas of roasting turkey, sweet potatoes, pickled vegetables, caper sauce and delectable apple and pumpkin pies wafted through the big house.

When we were all seated around the long oak table, Andrew's father asked for a blessing on the food, on our homes, our families and our friendships. After the meal the men settled in front of the fireplace with their cigars and pipes for an evening of conversation and chess. The ladies retreated to the music room to sing and play for one another. The first year I was to be included in the group of ladies, Andrew gave me my own collection of music, *Favorite Songs for the Piano*. I have it still, here in my treasure trunk.

Selecting a Christmas Tree

Each year during the first week of December, our horses
would be hitched to a sleigh and my father would cover
us with warm carriage wraps and drive the twenty miles
to the pine tree grove. As soon as we arrived, we would
run excitedly about, examining each pine whose height,
shape and scent had to please each member of the family.
My joy in the trip was doubled the year Andrew's family
began to join us on our search for the perfect tree. When
one had finally been chosen, my father would leave word
with the woodcutter as to which should be cut and
delivered to our home a few days before Christmas. On

our way back home we would always stop for a wonderful
supper at the Pine Lodge and, while our parents sipped
steaming cups of hot coffee, we children enjoyed the best
part of the entire adventure, ice skating under the stars
on the winding creek behind the lodge.

One year Andrew brought to our ice skating evening a
tiny pair of white fur muffs. Inside each one was a merry
silver bell. The muffs could be attached to my skates by
threading the skate lace through them. What a happy
sound! What a happy evening! What a happy memory
to bring with me! The little muffs still ring with the
joy of love and laughter. I have them still, here in my
treasure trunk.

Trimming the Tree

The day that the tree was to arrive, the entire household would ripple with impatient excitement. The girls would post themselves, expectantly, at the parlor window to watch for the woodcutter's wagon. The boys, too restless to remain indoors, would station themselves at the gate. When the tree finally arrived, the boys would help carry it into the house and set it up in its traditional place in the bay window of the parlor.

For days we had busied ourselves sorting through boxes of decorations brought down from the attic. Soon, the bare tree branches would begin to fill with lace snowflakes, satin bows, tiny crystal wreaths and angels —all kinds of angels, for I loved them best of all the ornaments. Grandmother's velvet-robed angel with the delicate porcelain face and hands always held the place of honor at the top of the tree. The last ornaments to be put in place were dozens of miniature white candles. For us, the Christmas season began when Mother would light each candle and bring the tree to life.

Of course, Andrew knew of my fondness for angels, and when he was old enough to handle a whittling knife, he carved a little wooden angel for me. It will be the first ornament to adorn the tree in our own home. I have it still, here in my treasure trunk.

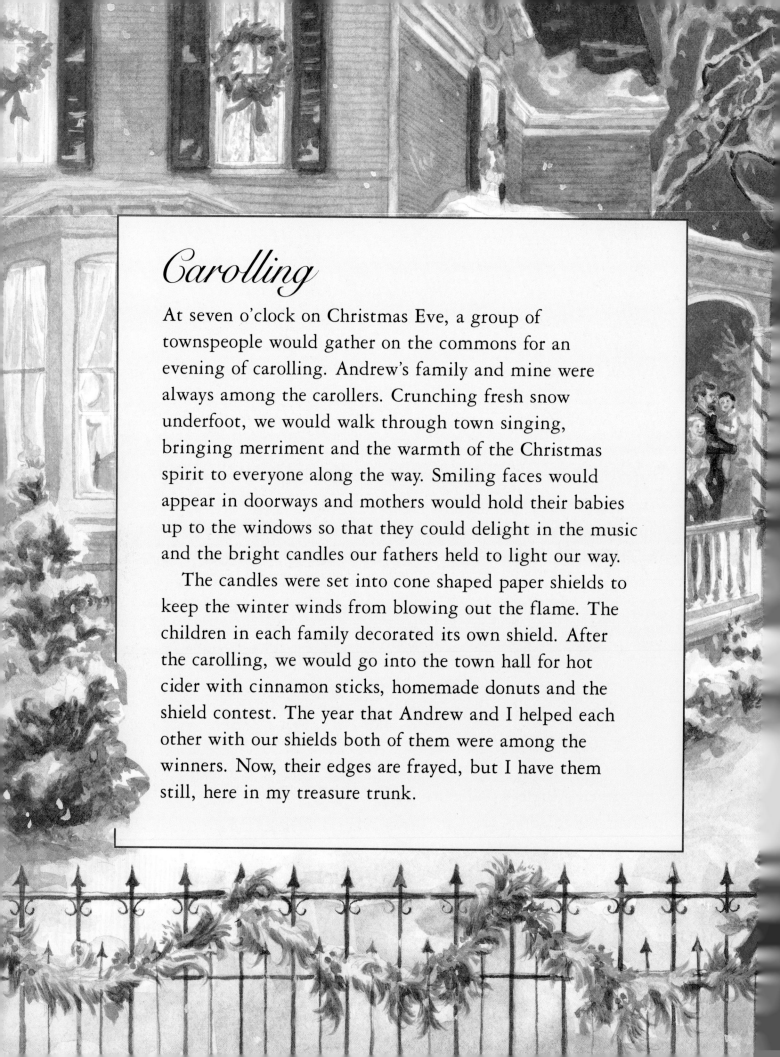

Carolling

At seven o'clock on Christmas Eve, a group of townspeople would gather on the commons for an evening of carolling. Andrew's family and mine were always among the carollers. Crunching fresh snow underfoot, we would walk through town singing, bringing merriment and the warmth of the Christmas spirit to everyone along the way. Smiling faces would appear in doorways and mothers would hold their babies up to the windows so that they could delight in the music and the bright candles our fathers held to light our way.

The candles were set into cone shaped paper shields to keep the winter winds from blowing out the flame. The children in each family decorated its own shield. After the carolling, we would go into the town hall for hot cider with cinnamon sticks, homemade donuts and the shield contest. The year that Andrew and I helped each other with our shields both of them were among the winners. Now, their edges are frayed, but I have them still, here in my treasure trunk.

Christmas Morning

Christmas morning in our home was the most joyous and exciting event of the year. The first child to rise would peep over the banister to see if Santa Claus had really come. Under the tree would be a mountain of brightly wrapped gifts. Shouts of "He came! He came!" would ring through the house and wake anyone who might still be sleeping. Soon, the entire family would be gathered in the parlor. In a moment we would all have new toys in our hands and the floor would sparkle with shiny crumpled paper, and with red, gold and green ribbon. Wicker cradles, porcelain dolls, hand-painted tea sets, rocking horses, lead soldiers, wooden trains, sleds and skates brought forth squeals of delight and admiration.

Mother, smiling happily, would slip into the kitchen. She knew the aroma of steaming chocolate and oven-hot apple, raisin and cinnamon cakes would eventually bring the girls hugging new dolls and the boys clutching a train engine or a handful of soldiers to breakfast.

Later, we would meet Andrew's family at the church service and they would come back to our home to exchange gifts and spend a merry day with us. Andrew would always have a special gift for me, one he had made or had shopped for himself. One of my favorites has always been a little locket in which he had put a photograph of the two of us. I have it still, here in my treasure trunk.

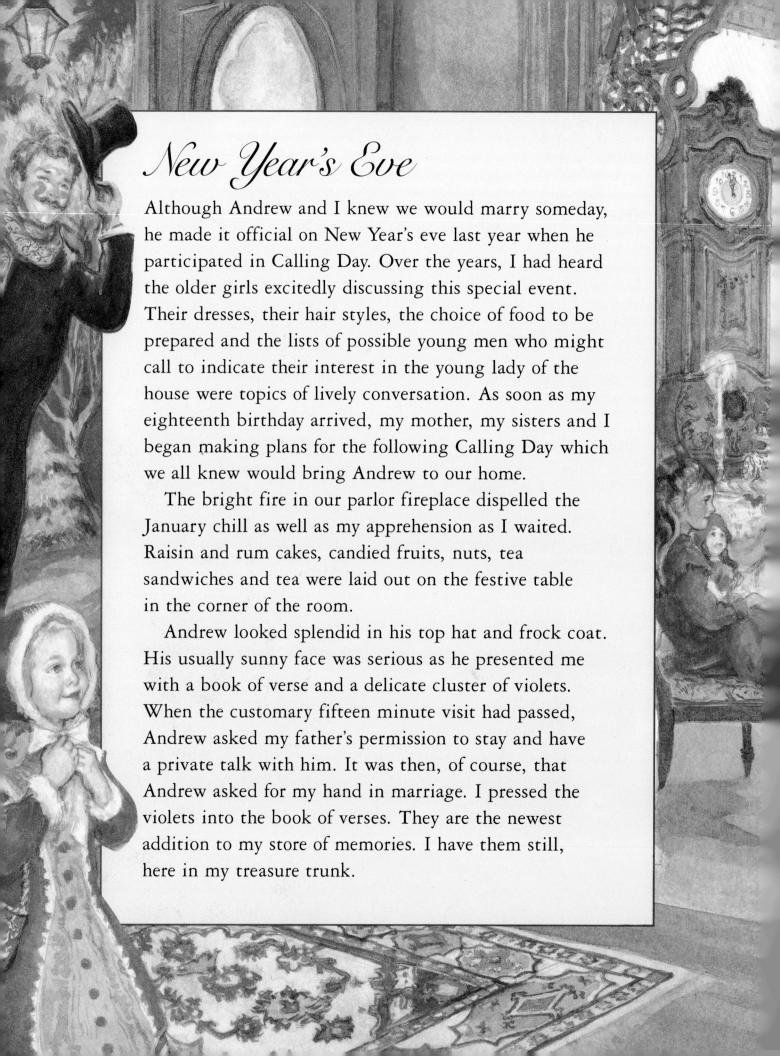

New Year's Eve

Although Andrew and I knew we would marry someday, he made it official on New Year's eve last year when he participated in Calling Day. Over the years, I had heard the older girls excitedly discussing this special event. Their dresses, their hair styles, the choice of food to be prepared and the lists of possible young men who might call to indicate their interest in the young lady of the house were topics of lively conversation. As soon as my eighteenth birthday arrived, my mother, my sisters and I began making plans for the following Calling Day which we all knew would bring Andrew to our home.

The bright fire in our parlor fireplace dispelled the January chill as well as my apprehension as I waited. Raisin and rum cakes, candied fruits, nuts, tea sandwiches and tea were laid out on the festive table in the corner of the room.

Andrew looked splendid in his top hat and frock coat. His usually sunny face was serious as he presented me with a book of verse and a delicate cluster of violets. When the customary fifteen minute visit had passed, Andrew asked my father's permission to stay and have a private talk with him. It was then, of course, that Andrew asked for my hand in marriage. I pressed the violets into the book of verses. They are the newest addition to my store of memories. I have them still, here in my treasure trunk.

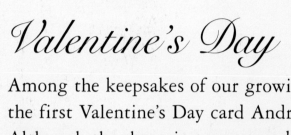

Valentine's Day

Among the keepsakes of our growing years I found
the first Valentine's Day card Andrew ever gave me.
Although the shops in town were brimming with
gorgeous cards, drawn and decorated by famous artists
of the day and costing extravagant amounts of money, I
thought Andrew's homemade card the most beautiful and
the most precious of any. The verse he composed still
brings tears of joy to my eyes each time I read the
childishly scrawled message:

> *Dear Elizabeth*
> *You are the flowers in the spring.*
> *You are the song the robins sing.*
> *For me the sun will always shine*
> *If you will be my Valentine.*
>
> > *Andrew*

How could we be married on any day but Valentine's
Day, we who have been sweethearts since the beginning
of time? The card is bent and yellowing, but still as
precious as the day I received it. I have it still, here in
my treasure trunk.

Our Wedding Day